How to Start carving

How to
Start carving

Charles Graveney

STUDIO VISTA London

 VAN NOSTRAND REINHOLD COMPANY New York

Acknowledgments

The author would like to thank David and Michael Goldsmith for posing for some of the photographs.
Colour photographs are by Peter Hirst-Smith.

A Studio Vista/Van Nostrand Reinhold How-to Book

Copyright © 1972 by Charles Graveney

Photoset, printed and bound in England by
BAS Printers Limited, Wallop, Hampshire

Published in Great Britain by
Studio Vista
Blue Star House, Highgate Hill, London N19
and in the United States by
Van Nostrand Reinhold Company
A Division of Litton Educational Publishing, Inc.
450 West 33rd Street, New York, N.Y. 10001.

Library of Congress Catalog Card Number 71–161976
ISBN 0 289 70193 7

Contents

Introduction

This book has been designed as a beginner's introduction to the art of woodcarving. Only the simplest of tools—a knife, a saw and a drill—are needed to make a wide variety of the items described. Simple, step-by-step instructions avoid the use of technical jargon.

Absolute beginners should start with the 'Simple woodcarving and whittling' section after first having read the opening pages on the selection of tools and materials.

Important
Although measurements have been given in both milli-metres and inches, the two sets of measurements are not interchangeable. Readers choosing to work in inches should use the measurements printed in parentheses for all tools, wood sizes, dowelling and listed instructions.

Tools for whittling and woodcarving

a knife
b tenon saw
c coping saw
d mitre block
e hand drill with twist bits
f small wood rasp
   riffler
   vice
   sandpaper
   clear polyurethane varnish
   cutting board
   G cramp (C clamp in U.S.A.)

Knives

There are special knives for chip-carving and whittling, with fixed and retractable blades.

A two-bladed pocket knife is good if the handle is strong, and the blades do not wobble when open.

A most useful and versatile tool is the craft knife. The X-acto no. 5 has a good firm handle and a large assortment of different shaped blades.

It is most important to select knives of the best quality steel and to keep them sharp.

A blunt tool is more dangerous than a sharp one.

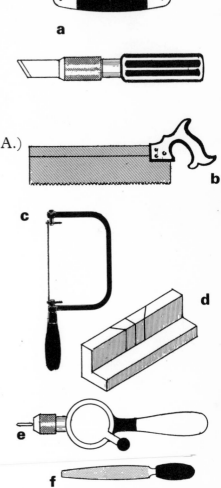

7

How to sharpen knives

A sharp knife can be kept in good condition for a short while by rubbing each side on fine emery paper laid on a flat surface, keeping the blade tilted at the cutting angle. A craft knife should be tilted at the angle of the bevel on the edge of the blade. If the tool is very blunt, then a fine grade oilstone should be used in place of the emery paper.

Cutting board

This should be of plywood about 12 mm. ($\frac{1}{2}$ in.) thick. It is used to protect a table surface when trimming outlines with a knife or chisel, or when drilling holes. Lay a sheet of sandpaper on it for smoothing flat work.

Sandpaper sticks and rifflers

Rifflers are small files shaped at each end and used for getting into awkward corners that are difficult to reach.

Sandpaper sticks are a great help in blending forms together after shaping with the knife. Make them from dowels about 15 cm. (or 6 in.) long and of various diameters, using different grades of paper, preferably garnet paper.

Cut the larger dowels down the centre to make half round ones. Roll the paper round the stick to find the correct width, cut to size, and cover both stick and the back of the paper with contact adhesive (Evo-Stik, or similar). Follow the maker's instructions for using the adhesive. Lay both paper and stick on a flat surface and, pressing firmly, roll the paper round the stick.

When sandpapering an undulating surface, wrap the sandpaper round a piece of expanded polystyrene, material used for packaging, and making ceiling tiles. It is more pliable than the usual cork or wood block.

Suitable woods

Most of the items illustrated in this book have been made from dowels and ready-planed strips of pine or whitewood, all easily obtainable from timber merchants (lumberyards) or hobby shops. Most hardware stores in America stock pine lath and hardwood dowel, as well as tools and glues.

Balsa wood is too soft for whittling or carving, and parana pine is too hard, unless used for chip carving. Douglas fir, pine and larch all have an interesting grain. Mahogany, walnut and jelutong are good, plain-coloured woods to use in contrast to those with a striped grain.

Branches pruned from apple and pear trees are good for whittling, but should be seasoned* for several months in a cool, airy place before use.

Finishing

Most woods require some kind of protective finish to prevent dust and grease from penetrating the grain.

A thin coat of clear polyurethane varnish is usually sufficient to protect the surface and show to advantage the natural grain markings.

Soft woods may be stained or dyed in many colours which are available, ready-mixed, from hobby shops.

For painting birds, animals or figures in natural colours, water colour paints are suitable if given a protective coat of varnish when dry.

Poster colours may be used on plain woods such as bass, lime and jelutong that have no attractive grain.

For a brilliant colour finish the small tins or bottles of enamel sold for model makers are ideal.

*see glossary page 67.

Tracing from a drawing

1 Lay a piece of tracing paper over the drawing you wish to copy, and carefully trace over the lines with a soft lead pencil

2 Remove the tracing paper from the drawing, lay it face down, and draw over the outline you have traced.

3 Turn the paper face up again and lay it on the wood where you want your drawing. It can be kept in position with masking tape.

4 Draw over the outline once more, pressing firmly. On lifting the paper you will find the drawing transferred to the wood.

Making a templet

If a tracing is used more than once it may wear thin or tear. A templet will last longer and be more accurate.

1 Make a tracing as before, but instead of tracing the outline onto the wood, transfer it onto thin card.

2 Cut round the outline with a knife or scissors and you will have a templet. Lay this on the wood in the required position and draw round the outline. This gives a cleaner line than tracing direct onto the wood.

A double-ended arrow on drawings or templets indicates the direction of the grain of the wood.

Soap carving

Soap is a material that is easily worked, clean to handle, and readily obtainable. It is not necessary to use the best quality soaps, and many stores sell bundles of slightly damaged tablets, often in a variety of shapes and colours, at a moderate price.

It is advisable to do the carving over a sheet of clean paper so as to collect the chips and shavings that fall. These can be used to repair damages and, of course, are still suitable to use for washing.

Although quite detailed work is possible in this material, the finished item should retain approximately the original shape of the tablet. It should not have any protrusions that are liable to be easily broken.

Useful tools
penknife or craft knife
metal nail file
varnish brush for cleaning away the shavings
coping saw for cutting outlines

Repairs
However careful you are, it is possible that small parts of your carving may be broken or damaged. Use some of the waste shavings to repair them. Mix them into a stiff paste with a very little water. Wet the broken area and, with the paste, build up a piece large enough to be carved into shape once it has dried.

If large pieces have been broken off, make a creamy paste with the shavings and, after wetting the broken areas, use the paste as a kind of glue. Squeeze the two parts together and allow them to dry hard.

If the break is clean and undamaged, then a quick-setting glue may be satisfactory.

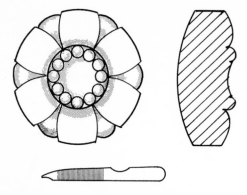

Flower
(colour photograph page 33)

A flower design is easily applied to a circular tablet.

1 Draw a circle in the centre of the tablet with compasses, or draw round a coin instead.

2 With a knife or nail file, shape the surface of the tablet as shown in the diagram of the section through the tablet.

3 Divide the circumference into six equal parts and draw the petals onto the soap.

4 With the point of the knife, cut out the triangles between the petals and finish shaping their outlines.

5 Divide the inner circle into an equal number of sections and carefully shape them into rounded stamens with the point of the nail file.

6 Brush clean.

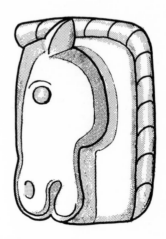

Horse's head (Photograph page 33)
This design has been simplified to fit into the shape of a square tablet and yet retain the main features of the animal. Do not try to include too much detail. A simple design often makes a more interesting composition than an attempt at a lifelike portrait. Compare this formal diagram with the more realistic example on page 33.

1 Trace the outline onto the tablet of soap.

2 Cut the area of the mane about 6 mm. ($\frac{1}{4}$ in.) below the top surface, leaving the ear solid.

3 Using the illustration as a guide, cut a chamfer* down the front of the nose, a V section round the cheek, and a radius* down the back of the neck.

4 Score in the hair lines and draw in the eye and mouth with the point of the nail file.

Words marked * are explained in the glossary on page 67.

Tortoise (Photograph page 33)

1 Draw the outline of your tortoise and make a templet as described on page 10. Use sticky tape to hold the templet in position on the soap while you draw round it with a pencil.

2 Flatten the underside of the tablet.

3 With the knife, gradually slice away the soap up to the outline. Do not try to take off too much with one cut (diagram a).

4 Cut the outline of the shell more deeply.

5 Cut the profiles of the head and legs, keeping the shapes square and solid (diagram b).

6 Use the knife to complete the shaping of the shell, occasionally brushing off the shavings to stop them sticking to the work.

7 Finish shaping the head and legs, and chamfer the underside of the shell.

8 Draw or trace the sections on the back of the shell and mark them in with the point of the nail file.

9 With the same tool, draw in the details of the eyes, mouth and toes.

10 Brush clean.

a

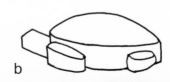

b

c

Tropical fish

1 Draw your fish's outline onto the tablet of soap.

2 Cut round the outline with a saw blade or knife.

3 Make a cut about 6 mm. ($\frac{1}{4}$ in.) deep in the side of the tablet all round the outline of the body. Shave the tail and fins down towards it. Turn the tablet over and shave the other side down too.

4 Cut a chamfer all round the body and head (see photograph).

5 Cut a line round the gills, and shape the nose and mouth.

6 With the point of the knife or nail file finish drawing the outline of the tail and fin.

7 Shape the hollows in the tail and fins with the round end of the nail file.

8 Smooth the body and head and then draw on the scales and the eye and mouth details with the point of the file.

9 Last of all cut through the hole between the tail and fins, leaving them joined together at the ends for strength.

Simple woodcarving and whittling

Helicopter
You need:
penknife or craft knife
lath or soft wood 12 × 2 cm. × 5 mm. ($4\frac{3}{4}$ × $\frac{3}{4}$ × $\frac{1}{4}$ in.)
dowel 3 mm. ($\frac{1}{8}$ in.) diameter, 18 cm. (7 in.) long
drill 3 mm. ($\frac{1}{8}$ in.) diameter
cutting board and fixing button
sandpaper; glue

1 Measure the exact length of the lath, divide by two, and draw a line across the centre.

2 Repeat this operation across the width, to find the exact centre of the lath.

3 With the point of your knife, scribe* a small dimple where the two lines cross. This is to mark where the hole is to be drilled. It also helps to prevent the drill point from moving out of position. You should do this before any drilling operation.

4 Fix the work on the cutting board with a clamp or button. This will stop the wood revolving while the hole is being drilled, **a**. Drill a hole through the centre.

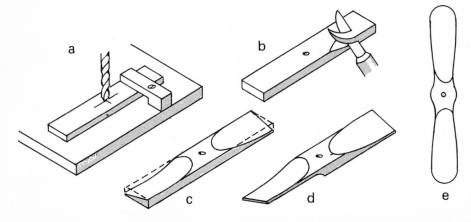

5 Shape one half of the blade as shown in diagram **b**. Make the cut on the slant so that the far side of the lath is left at its full thickness and the near side is shaved away almost completely (diagram **b**).

6 Shape the other side of the blade so that it slopes in the opposite direction (diagram **c**). Leave a flat area of about 20 mm. ($\frac{3}{4}$ in.) diameter in the centre.

7 Turn the blade over and repeat the shaping (diagram **d**). Reduce the blade to a thickness of 2 mm. ($\frac{1}{16}$ in.).

8 Cut to the outline shown in diagram **e**.

9 Test for balance. Place the blade on a pin so that it can spin freely. If one side is heavier than the other, gradually trim down the thickness. At the end of a spin an evenly balanced blade will settle in a horizontal position.

10 Sandpaper smooth. Glue in the dowel, making sure that it is square with the blade.

The helicopter is operated by holding the dowel between the hands, then rubbing the right hand briskly forward and releasing the dowel. The helicopter will spin and rise straight up.

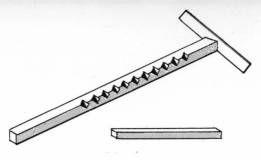

Yes-No stick

You need:

parana pine strip 25 cm. × 8 × 8 mm. (10 × $\frac{3}{8}$ × $\frac{3}{8}$ in.)
parana pine strip 15 cm. × 8 × 8 mm. (6 × $\frac{3}{8}$ × $\frac{3}{8}$ in.)
plywood strip or lath 10 cm. × 18 × 3 mm. (4 × $\frac{3}{4}$ × $\frac{1}{8}$ in.)
knife; saw; drill
nail 2 cm. ($\frac{3}{4}$ in.) long

The Yes-No stick is sometimes called a lie detector and is a useful addition to any witchdoctor's tool kit. When the owner is asked a question he must rub the stick briskly with the shorter one. If the true answer is yes, the end will spin in a clockwise direction. If the answer is no, the blade will spin in the other direction.

1 Take the longer pine strip and cut notches along one edge (see drawing). Space them about 12 mm. ($\frac{1}{2}$ in.) apart.

2 Drill a hole in the centre of the lath. Nail it centrally to the end of the notched stick. The blade should be balanced and spin freely.

The secret of the stick is in the skill of the operator. Grasp the longer stick firmly in the left hand with the notches facing you. Rub the short stick back and forth across the notches.

To make the blade turn clockwise, the forefinger of the right hand holding the short stick must be held underneath the notched stick and press upwards.

To turn the blade in the opposite direction, the fore-finger must be kept out of the way. Instead, the thumb of the right hand should be pressed against the front face of the notched stick while the short stick is rubbed back and forth across the notches.

Counters

Checkers, draughts, or the Ladies' Game, as it is known in many European countries, is one of the most popular games played with counters. Twenty-four pieces are needed for it; twelve remaining the natural light colour of the wood, and twelve dyed a contrasting colour.

You need:
tenon saw
mitre block with stop gauge
piece of broom handle 25 cm. (10 in.) long
wood dye
clear varnish
sandpaper, coarse and fine

The mitre block is usually L-shaped, and it is a good idea to glue an extra strip of wood along the front edge of it. This will fit over the edge of the table and stop the block slipping about when in use. A stop gauge is used for cutting a number of pieces of equal length. It is a block of wood set at the required distance from the saw line and held in position with a screw or G cramp (called a C clamp in America).

1 Set the stop gauge on the mitre block 9 mm. ($\frac{3}{8}$ in.) from the saw line. Hold the wood firmly in the mitre block, with one end of it against the stop gauge.

2 Saw through the wood with a smooth even stroke. Use just sufficient pressure for the teeth to cut. A good clean saw cut will mean less time spent in finishing. Saw off twenty-three more pieces.

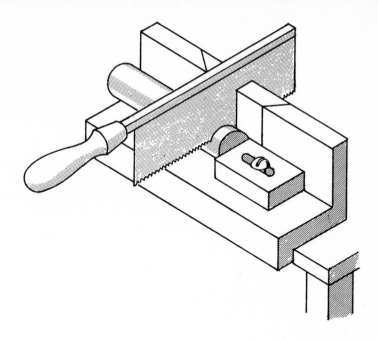

3 Lay a sheet of coarse sandpaper on a flat surface and rub each side of the counters across it to remove the saw marks. Then smooth them with fine sandpaper.

4 Varnish twelve of the pieces. Stain the others with wood dye and sandpaper them again before varnishing. *Follow the maker's instructions when using stains or varnishes.*

Spinning top
You need:

plywood 70 × 70 × 4 mm. ($2\frac{3}{4}$ × $2\frac{3}{4}$ × $\frac{1}{8}$ in.)
dowel 6 mm. ($\frac{1}{4}$ in.) diameter, 5 cm. (2 in.) long
tenon saw; knife

6 mm. ($\frac{1}{4}$ in.) drill
compasses; pencil
ruler; glue
sandpaper
paints and brush

1 Draw a circle on the plywood. Divide the circle into six parts by drawing three diagonals through the

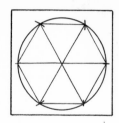

centre, as when cutting up a pie. Draw the diagonals lightly at first, and experiment until the six parts are as equal as you can get them.

2 Draw straight lines to join the points on the circumference. Holding the work against the mitre block, saw along the lines.

3 Fix the work down and drill a hole through the centre. Sandpaper it smooth and clean.

4 Sharpen the end of the dowel to a point and push it through the hole. Spin the top to test it. Adjust the position of the dowel if necessary, before glueing it in position.

5 Paint each segment with a different colour and number them from one to six with figures or spots.

This top may be used in place of a die for Ludo or Snakes and Ladders.

Whistle
You need:
bamboo stick between 15–20 mm. ($\frac{5}{8}$–$\frac{3}{4}$ in.) diameter wooden dowel; saw; knife; round file; sandpaper

1 Saw through the bamboo 10 cm. (4 in.) from a

knuckle. Saw through the knuckle so that this end of the piece is solid.

2 File the inside of the open end smooth and round, and select a length of dowel that is a close fit inside the hole for a depth of 25 mm. (1 in.).

3 At 25 mm. (1 in.) from the open end of the bamboo make a saw cut down to about one third of the thickness. With the saw or knife make a sloping cut to meet the first cut at an angle of about 60 degrees, **a**.

4 Cut a flat on the dowel to reduce its diameter very slightly, **b**. Insert it into the bamboo until the end is level with the saw cut, keeping the flat surface uppermost, **c**.

5 Try blowing down the mouthpiece. If you get no sound, vary the angle of the notch cut or increase the width of the flat on the dowel until satisfactory. A longer piece of bamboo will give a higher note.

6 Saw off the protruding end of the dowel and cut off the mouthpiece at an angle, **d**.

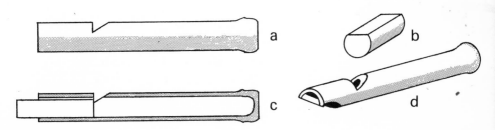

Chip carving

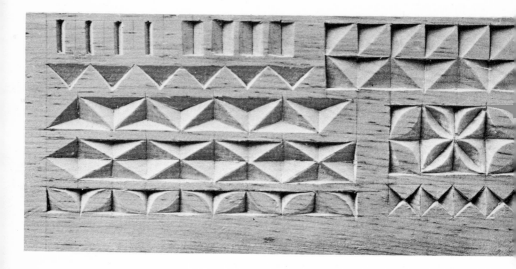

This is a name given to a craft that has been practised in most countries and over many centuries. Examples are to be found from Egypt to Iceland. It has been used to decorate tombs, furniture, barn doors, boxes, spoons, spinning wheels, and ginger bread moulds.

Although there is no limit to the infinite variety of designs that can be achieved with chip-carving, there are only a few basic cuts. These consist mainly of notches incised in the surface of the wood.

Practise the simple cuts in soft wood before decorating an item you have made.

You need:
skew-ended craft knife or spade chisel
soft wood 1 cm. ($\frac{3}{8}$ in.) thick (pine, lime, whitewood, African walnut, or similar even-textured wood)

The single-faced triangle

1 Draw a line parallel with the top edge of the wood.

2 Along this draw a line of right-angled triangles with diagonal base lines about 6 mm. ($\frac{1}{4}$ in.) long.

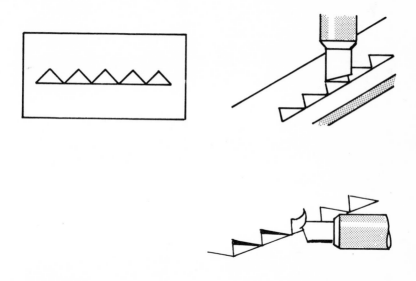

3 Holding the knife vertically along one side of the triangle, insert the point at the apex of the triangle. Press down firmly along the line. The aim is to make a vertical cut that is deepest at the apex of the triangle and tapers off to nothing at the base.

4 Make a similar cut on the other side of the triangle. Repeat these cuts all along the line of triangles.

25

5 Hold the knife at a low angle to the wood and, if you are right-handed, start your cut at the right-hand side of the triangle. Cut down towards the corner and finish the cut on the left-hand side of the triangle. This should remove the chip quite cleanly. If not, do not try to dig it out, but cut the two sides of the triangle a little deeper and try again.

If the base of the triangle does not come out level along your pencil line, it means the knife is not held at the correct angle. Continue this cut on the other triangles. By the time you reach the end of the row, you should have got the angle correct.

Variations
Carve a row of triangles below the first ones, using the same base line but with the apex of the triangles pointing downwards.

Then try a row at right angles to these, across the grain.

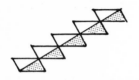

The two-faced triangle

This is really two single-faced triangles joined together. In this case the deepest point is where the apexes of the two triangles meet at **a**. The bases af the two triangles are not side by side but form a right angle to each other.

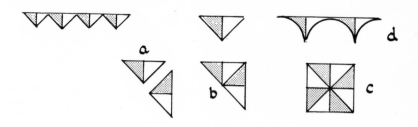

Two of these two-faced triangles can be joined at right angles to produce design **b**. Point **b** is the highest point, as this is where the base lines of the triangles meet.

It is now a simple matter to complete the square by adding a repeat of pattern **b** to produce design **c**. The centre of the square is the highest point.

Variation

Try removing the chip of triangle **a** with a curved action of the tool to produce a radius on the surface of the wood, as at **d**.

Three-faced triangle

Draw a right-angled triangle with a base of about 1.5 cm. ($\frac{5}{8}$ in.) and make vertical cuts from the centre to each corner, deep in the centre and fading out to the corners. Cut out the chips as for the other triangles.

Paper knife 1
You need:
skew-ended craft knife or spade chisel
sandpaper, coarse and fine
pine lath or any straight, close-grained wood
    20 cm. × 25 × 4 mm. (8 × 1 × $\frac{1}{4}$ in.)

1 Draw the outline of the knife on the wood.

2 Use a knife to shape the wood close to the outline.

3 From a point where the decoration will end, shave the wood away towards the cutting edge.

4 Round off all sharp edges and finish shaping with coarse sandpaper, following with fine sandpaper to give a soft smooth finish.

5 Draw the pattern onto the handle, starting with a guide line parallel with the edge and a little way inside it.

6 Cut the pattern of single and double-faced triangles. (See pages 24–27 for detailed instructions.)

7 Finish with three coats of clear varnish. Let each coat dry and rub it down with fine sandpaper before applying the next.

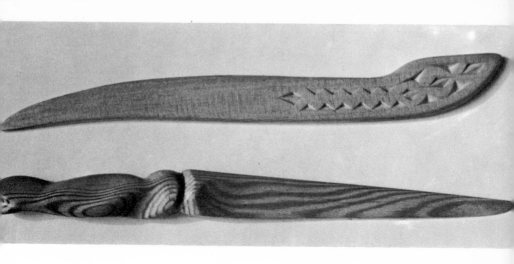

Paper knife 2

You need:
half round wood rasp
sandpaper, coarse and fine
clear varnish
wood with a strong grain
    pattern. Annual rings
    should run diagonally
    across the end grain of
    the wood (see diagram).
    size 20 × 1.8 × 1.2 cm.
    (8 × $\frac{3}{4}$ × $\frac{1}{2}$ in.)

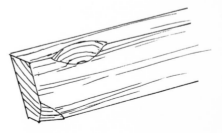

This knife of abstract design makes use of the strong grain markings in the wood. The annual rings of the tree form interesting patterns when the surface of the wood is made to undulate. It is possible to exercise a certain amount of control over the design by varying the depth and direction of the carving.

The wood may be held in a vice, or you may hold it in your hand and rest it on the edge of the bench or table.

1 Use a rasp to remove all sharp corners from the handle end of the knife.

2 With the round face of the rasp make one or two hollow grooves diagonally across the edge of the wood.

3 Make similar, though not identical, grooves on the other side of the handle.

4 Make the outline of the handle irregular, but of a shape that feels comfortable to hold. At this point you will see the darker lines in the wood beginning to form a distinct pattern. Regulate this by varying the depth and direction of the cut.

5 Use coarse sandpaper to blend the forms together and soften the outlines.

6 With the knife and rasp, gradually taper the blade from the handle to a point at the tip. Shape the blade to a wedge-shaped section towards the cutting edge.

7 Finish with clear varnish as for paper knife 1.

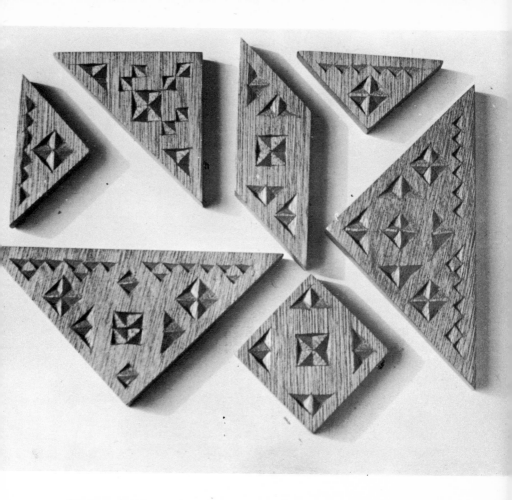

Tangrams

Tangrams are wisdom puzzles that originated in China, where they were beautifully carved in ivory. The English name may well be derived from the two words 'tangent' and 'anagram'; for the pieces may be arranged in hundreds of different ways, each making a picture or diagram.

Tangrams are made up of seven pieces: five triangles, a square, and a rhomboid. They are ideal for decorating with chip-carving.

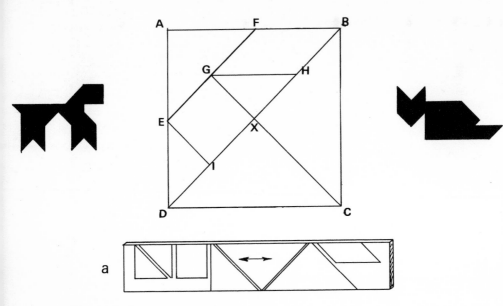

You need:
tenon saw; mitre block
craft knife with chisel end 1 cm. ($\frac{3}{8}$ in.) wide
sheet of thin card; pencil; scissors
sandpaper, coarse and fine
clear varnish and brush
close-grained wood without strong markings, planed
on both sides and edges, 30 × 5 cm. × 9 mm.
(12 × 2 × $\frac{3}{8}$ in.)

1 Draw a 10 cm. (4 in.) square on the card. Draw a line from B to D. Mark the middle point of lines AB and AD. Join EF and GC. Mark the middle point of DX and XB. Join EI and GH (see above).

2 Cut along the lines to make the templets.

3 Lay the templets on the wood as in diagram **a** and draw round the outlines. Use the edges of the wood as a location for each piece. Leave sufficient space for a saw cut between the pieces.

4 Use the mitre block to hold the wood accurately in position and saw off each part close to the line.

5 Clean up all the sawn edges to size by rubbing them on a sheet of coarse sandpaper laid on a flat surface.

6 Finish all surfaces and edges with fine sandpaper.

7 Give a thin coat of clear varnish all over.

The carved design illustrated is composed entirely of single and two-faced triangles as described on pages 25–27. The design should be drawn on the wood in pencil before you start to cut.

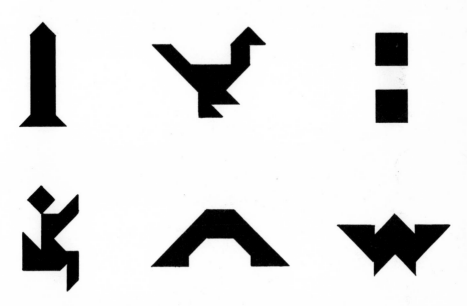

You can build up all these shapes—and hundreds more —from one tangram. (Solutions on page 66)

Pastry roller

You need:
wooden cotton reel or spool
6 mm. ($\frac{1}{4}$ in.) dowel 6 cm. ($2\frac{1}{4}$ in.)
    long
20 mm. ($\frac{3}{4}$ in.) dowel 4 cm.
    ($1\frac{1}{2}$ in.) long
skew-ended craft knife
6 mm. ($\frac{1}{4}$ in.) drill; tenon saw
sandpaper; glue; pencil

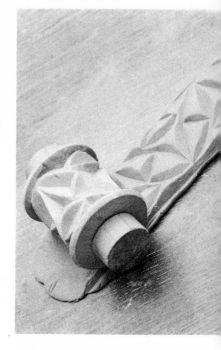

1 Divide the circumference
of the cotton reel or spool
into four equal sections.
Using these marks as a
guide, draw four vertical
lines from top to bottom of
the reel.

2 Draw a diagonal line between each pair of vertical
lines, **a**.

3 Draw the leaf shape on each diagonal, **b**.

4 Draw the diamond in the centre of each leaf shape, **c**.

5 Draw the horizontal leaf shape between each section, **d**

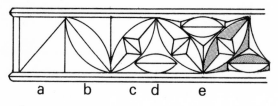

a   b   c d   e

36

6 Draw in the centre lines of the triangle between the leaf shapes, **e**.

The cuts must be made fairly deeply, so it is best to hold the work in a vice. With the exception of the leaf shape, the design is based on the three-faced triangle, as described in page 27.

7 First carve the diagonal leaf shapes, setting in with the knife or chisel the centre lines of the triangle. Cut out each section, gradually making the cuts deeper until they follow the line of the drawing, **c**.

8 Cut out the smaller leaf shapes. Make a straight cut down each centre line and a sloping cut from each side to meet it.

9 Finally, cut the small triangles between the leaf shapes. These are the three-faced triangles.

10 Drill a hole through the centre of the thicker dowel and saw it in half.

11 Remove the labels from the ends of the cotton reel or spool and sandpaper smooth.

12 Glue one piece of the thicker dowel on the end of the thinner one. Push it through the reel and glue the second thicker piece on the other end. Leave enough clearance for the reel to spin freely. When the glue is dry, trim off any protruding ends of the spindle and sandpaper them smooth.

The roller is used by holding the spindle between the thumb and forefinger and rolling it over the pastry.

Scrolls

Many different countries and civilizations have found the scroll a most useful decorative form. The following pages illustrate a few ways in which one motif can be multiplied and arranged to produce a variety of designs (see also page 34).

Try making several scrolls, painting them in different colours and arranging them on a variety of backgrounds. Choose the best design and glue the scrolls in position.

You need:
pine lath about 1 m. × 24 × 4 mm. (36 × 1 × ⅛ in.)
coping saw or fretsaw
knife
sandpaper, coarse and fine
varnish or paints

1 Trace the scroll from the diagram and make templets in thin card. Use them to draw about 20 scrolls on the wood.

2 Draw on to the wood several circles with the same diameter as that of the scroll end. Find a coin the right size to use as a templet.

3 Cut out the scrolls and circles with the coping saw. Trim the edges with the knife.

4 Sandpaper the edges and both faces. Paint or varnish the pieces.

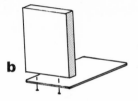

a   **b**

Book ends (colour photograph page 34)
You need:
two pieces of wood 14 × 10 × 1.5 cm. (5½ × 4 × ½ in.)
two pieces of plywood 10 × 10 cm. × 3 mm.
   (4 × 4 × ⅛ in.)
a number of scrolls and circles to suit your design
glue; sandpaper; clear varnish

Any well-seasoned wood is suitable for the thicker pieces. Veneered plywood could also be used if the unsightly edges are painted.

1 With the coarse sandpaper make a small chamfer all round the front edges of the thick pieces of wood on which the design is to be glued.

2 Sandpaper all surfaces smooth.

3 Brush a coat of varnish all over. Allow to dry. Rub down with fine sandpaper and varnish once more.

4 Glue the scrolls and circles in position according to the design you have chosen. Allow to dry.

5 The sharp tip of the scrolls should be gradually tapered down to the background with a knife, **a**. Touch up the tips with paint or varnish.

6 Glue the thin ply to the bottom edge of the uprights. Secure it in position with two small nails or panel pins, **b**

Picture frame

You need skill and the right equipment to make a good mitred joint. Unless you have acquired both, why not purchase a frame ready made. Diagram **a** shows a plain moulding suitable for decorating with scrolls.

The frame in the photograph on page 34 was made with this moulding in the dimensions given below.

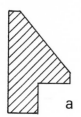 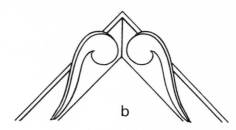

You need:
natural wood frame made from 1 in. moulding, inside
    dimensions 25 × 20 cm. (10 × 8 in.)
8 wood scrolls as described on page 38
fine sandpaper; quick-setting glue; clear varnish

1 Sandpaper all parts clean and smooth. Varnish them, allow them to dry, and sandpaper them once more.

2 Glue the scrolls to the frame, **b**.

3 Remove surplus glue. Do this before the glue has set, by sprinkling a little sawdust over it and scraping it away with the point of a knife.

4 Give a final coat of varnish if required.

Candle holders 1

You need:
wooden ball, diameter
   3 cm. ($1\frac{1}{4}$ in.)
wooden ball, diameter
   3.8 cm. ($1\frac{1}{2}$ in.)
tenon saw; vice
6 mm. ($\frac{1}{4}$ in.) drill
knife; glue; pencil
sandpaper, coarse and fine
plastic wood, natural colour
silver paint and brush

1 Draw a line round the centre of each ball.

2 Holding one of the balls in a vice, saw carefully round the centre line, gradually deepening the cut until the ball is in two equal halves. Cut the other ball in the same way.

3 Rub the flat surfaces smooth on a sheet of coarse sandpaper.

42

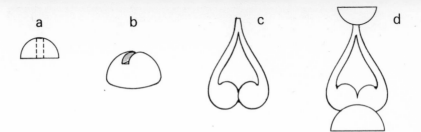

4 Drill a hole through the centre of the smaller halves, **a**.

5 In the centre of the round surface of the larger halves, saw a slot the width of the scrolls, **b**.

6 Trim the bottom of the slot with the knife, and finish with sandpaper, or file until the scrolls are a tight fit in the slot.

7 Glue two scrolls together at the edges, **c**, and allow to dry.

8 Glue the scrolls into the slot of the base, **d**, and allow to dry.

9 Remove the sharp edges on the points of the scrolls until they are a tight fit in the hole in part **a**. Glue in position and allow to dry. Clean up the joints with the knife and remove surplus glue before painting the candle holders silver (photograph page 34).

Candle holders 2

Use a large wooden cotton reel or spool, **a**. Saw off both ends. Sandpaper the surfaces and then saw a shallow slot across the centre of each, **b**. It should be just wide enough to take the scroll. Fit the scroll in the slot so that the top surface of the candle holder is level when the scroll is in position, **c**. Glue in position. Paint silver.

More advanced carving and whittling

Swan and cygnets
For the swan you need:
white pine, ready-planed, 20 × 8 × 1.2 cm.
   (8 × 3¼ × ½ in.)
coping saw or tenon saw
knife; half round rasp
tracing paper; thin card; scissors
pencil; UHU or other quick-setting glue
sandpaper sticks and a sheet of sandpaper
clear varnish and brush

1 Trace the outlines on the facing page and make templets of the four parts of the swan. (You need two templets of part **b**).

2 Lay the templets to the edge of the wood like this and draw round them.

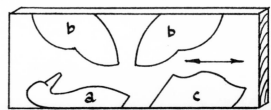

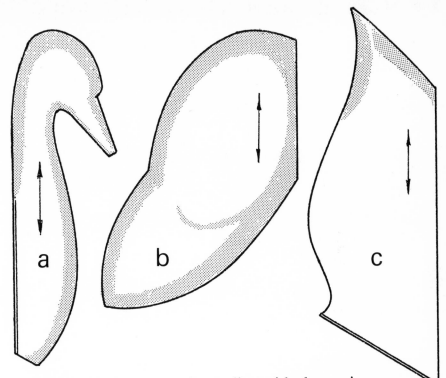

3 Saw round close to the outline with the coping saw or use a tenon saw to separate the parts and cut off the corners.

4 With the knife cut close to the outline.

5 Shape the body piece, **c**. Just taper the tail to a point at the tip, as shaded on the diagram.

6 Now shape the head and neck, **a**. Cut a small chamfer all round the neck and head as shown by the shaded outline, not touching that part where there are double lines, as these indicate a joint. Taper the beak to a point.

7 Cut a broad chamfer round the edges of the wing pieces, **b**, and where indicated by shading. Shape the tips of the wings like those in the photograph. Do not forget to shape one wing for the right side and one for the left.

8 Use sandpaper sticks to remove all tool marks and to give a soft finish.

9 Smooth and clean the joints by rubbing them on a sheet of sandpaper laid on a flat surface.

10 Glue the neck to the body.

11 When the first joint has dried, glue the wings in position. Each one should just touch the joint line of the neck (see photograph).

12 When the glue has set hard, rub the whole swan lightly with fine sandpaper.

13 Give your finished model a coat of clear varnish.

For the cygnets you need:
tenon saw; knife or flat chisel; rasp; sandpaper
UHU (or other quick-setting glue); mitre block
piece of broom handle 12 cm. ($4\frac{1}{2}$ in.) long with
    squared-up ends
dowel 18 mm. ($\frac{3}{4}$ in.) diameter, 3 cm. ($1\frac{1}{4}$ in.) long

The cygnets are carved together and separated on completion.

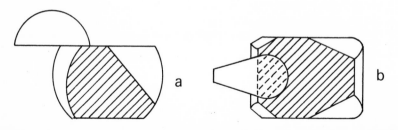

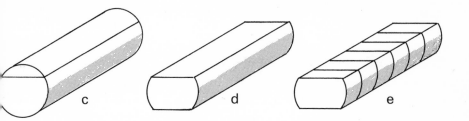

c   d   e

1 Draw a straight line across the ends of the broom handle and continue down each side (see diagram **c**).

2 Saw down the length of this line leaving sufficient clearance for finishing. Clean the surface with a rasp.

3 Still with the rasp, make a flat surface on the opposite side of the wood to reduce the overall thickness to 16 mm. ($\frac{5}{8}$ in.), **d**. Sandpaper smooth.

4 Divide the length into six equal parts. Using the mitre block, make a shallow saw cut round each division. Do not separate the pieces, **e**.

5 Make a templet of the shaded area in **b**. Use it for drawing chamfers on each section, **f** (see page 48).

6 Make a templet of the shaded area in **a**. Use it for back view, **h**, of each section.

7 Draw the chamfers on the front view, **g**, and on the back view, **h**, of each section.

8 Holding the work in a vice, cut the chamfers to the lines drawn using a knife or chisel.

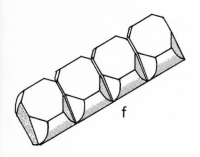

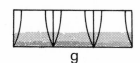

f

g

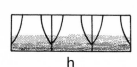

h

j

9 Use the mitre block to help you saw off each section. Sandpaper the edges of each piece.

10 For the heads, saw the dowel in half down the centre. Divide each half into three pieces, **j**.

11 Shape each piece to the outline on view **b**.

12 Sandpaper each head flat and smooth before glueing it in position, **b**.

Woodpecker
You need:
coping saw; knife; drill 6 mm. ($\frac{1}{4}$ in.) diameter
soft wood strip 15 × 5 × 1.4 cm. (6 × 2 × $\frac{5}{8}$ in.)
soft wood strip 12 × 3 × 1 cm. (4$\frac{3}{4}$ × 1$\frac{1}{4}$ × $\frac{3}{8}$ in.)
hardwood strip 12 × 3 cm. × 6 mm. (4$\frac{3}{4}$ × 1$\frac{1}{4}$ × $\frac{1}{4}$ in.)
dowel 6 mm. ($\frac{1}{4}$ in.) diameter, 6 cm. (2$\frac{3}{8}$ in.) long
piece of wood with bark 2 cm. ($\frac{3}{4}$ in.) diameter, 12 cm. (5 in.) long
sandpaper; glue; paints

1 Trace the outline of the bird, **a**, onto the larger soft wood strip and the two wings, **b**, onto the smaller one. (See diagrams on page 50)

2 Saw round the outlines with the coping saw.

3 Drill a hole 12 mm. ($\frac{1}{2}$ in.) deep in the centre of the breast of the bird, where indicated.

4 With a knife cut a chamfer all round the outline of the bird. Narrow the area round the neck, and finish shaping with sandpaper. Leave flat the area inside the dotted line.

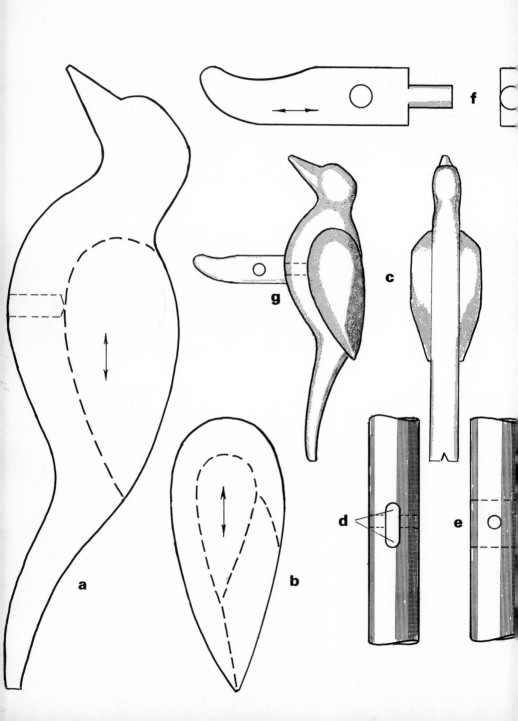

a

b

c

d

e

f

g

5 Cut the chamfers on the wings. Use diagram **c** and the dotted line on diagram **b** as guides. Sandpaper them and glue them in position.

6 Drill a hole about 7 cm. ($2\frac{3}{4}$ in.) from the top of the 'tree'. Drill a second hole 16 mm. ($\frac{5}{8}$ in.) below it. With the knife, cut away the wood between the holes to make a slot. Finish smooth with a rasp or sandpaper stick.

7 Turn the 'tree' sideways and drill a hole, **e**, through the middle of the slot and at right angles to it, dotted line, **d**.

8 Sandpaper the hardwood strip, **f**, and round off the edges until it fits freely through the slot.

9 Shape one end of the strip into a lever. At the other end, in the centre, cut a tenon* 6 mm. ($\frac{1}{4}$ in.) wide. Shape it round like a dowel until it is a tight fit in the hole in the breast of the bird, **g**.

10 Fit the lever through the slot so that the bird is close to the tree. Make a pencil mark on the lever through the hole in the side of the tree. Remove the lever from the bird and drill a hole where marked. Glue the lever back into the bird and leave to dry.

11 Fit the lever back through the slot and insert the dowel through the holes. If the movement is too tight, open up the slot or enlarge the hole in the lever.

12 Sandpaper all parts smooth and paint the bird.

Press the lever to make the bird peck at the tree.

D

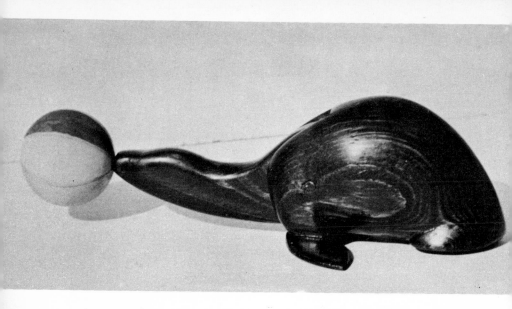

Performing sea lion

You need:

pine strip 30 × 7 × 1.2 cm. (12 × 2¾ × ½ in.)
wooden ball 3 cm. (1¼ in.) diameter
lath 6 × 2.5 cm × 4 mm. (2⅜ × 1 × ⅛ in.)
dowel 3 mm. (⅛ in.) diameter, 10 cm. (4 in.) long
coping saw; knife; 3 mm. (⅛ in.) drill; sandpaper
varnish; thin string or cord 20 cm. (8 in.) long
vice; glue; half round rasp; nail; wood stain

1 Trace parts **a**, **b** (twice) and **c** onto the pine. Mark the position of the holes. Trace part **d** onto the lath.

2 Hold the wood in a vice and cut round the outlines with the coping saw. Drill the holes.

3 Assemble the parts. Push the dowel through the holes to check that they line up accurately.

4 Enlarge the hole in part **a** with your next largest drill, so that it can move freely on the dowel.

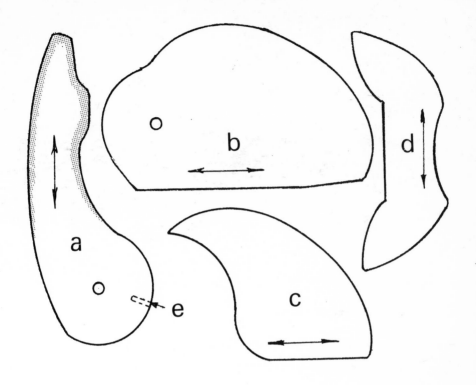

5 Glue together parts **b** and **c**. Leave the dowel in the holes to keep the parts in alignment. Leave to set.

6 Remove the dowel. Holding the work in a vice, start shaping the body, using the photograph as a guide. Remove the bulk of the wood with the knife and finish shaping with the rasp. Note how the rear flippers are indicated with a notch cut and finished with the rasp.

7 Shape the head and neck, **a**. Round all edges with the rasp, leaving the circular area flat. Sandpaper smooth and clean.

8 Glue the front flippers in position. Shape when dry.

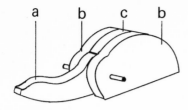

9 Put the head in position. Check that it moves freely. If it does not drop down horizontally, trim away the inside of the front flippers until it does.

10 Remove the head and drill a hole on the back edge of the neck at **e**. Glue in one end of the piece of string. Plug with a short piece of dowel.

11 Stain all the parts and varnish them.

12 Drill a small hole in the end of the nose, and another through the centre of the ball.

13 Paint the ball in various coloured segments.

14 Assemble the neck, dropping the string down through the body and out by the tail. Push the dowel through the body and neck and trim off the ends.

15 Fix the ball in position with a nail which should be glued into the end of the nose.

A pull on the string will make the head rise (see cover photograph).

Baby clown

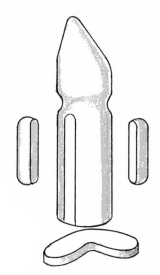

You need:
piece of broom handle
   9 cm. ($3\frac{1}{2}$ in.) long
dowel 1 cm. ($\frac{3}{8}$ in.) diameter,
   6 cm. ($2\frac{3}{8}$ in.) long
pine lath 5 × 2.5 cm. × 5 mm.
   (2 × 1 × $\frac{1}{4}$ in.)
tenon saw; rasp; sandpaper
mitre block; glue; paints

1 Hold the broom handle in the mitre block and saw off one end at 45 degrees. With the rasp, round off the point into a cone shape.

2 Draw a line for the neck 4 cm. ($1\frac{1}{2}$ in.) from the point of the cone. Make a groove all round with the rasp.

3 Rasp a flat surface about 5 mm. ($\frac{1}{4}$ in.) wide down each side.

4 Rasp a flat surface the same width down one side of the dowel and sandpaper it smooth. Saw it in half and round off the ends with rasp or sandpaper.

5 Draw the shape of the feet on the pine lath. Saw them roughly to shape and trim with the rasp.

6 Sandpaper all parts smooth before gluing them together. Remove surplus glue and allow to dry.

7 Paint the clown (see cover photograph).

Clown (see photograph on cover)
You need:
dowel, thick 18 mm. × 24 cm. ($\frac{3}{4}$ × $9\frac{1}{2}$ in.)
     medium 6 mm. × 10 cm. ($\frac{1}{4}$ × 4 in.)
     thin 3 mm. × 10 cm. ($\frac{1}{8}$ × 4 in.)
pinewood strip 10 × 6 × 1.2 cm. (4 × $2\frac{1}{2}$ × $\frac{1}{2}$ in.)
lath 24 × 2.5 cm. × 3 mm. ($9\frac{1}{2}$ × 1 × $\frac{1}{8}$ in.)
tenon saw; knife; rasp
drills 3 mm. ($\frac{1}{8}$ in.) and 6 mm. ($\frac{1}{4}$ in.) diameter
sandpaper; paints; vice

1 The head. Saw off a piece of thick dowel 6 cm.
($2\frac{1}{2}$ in.) long. Saw off one end at an angle and shape it
round with the rasp, **a**.

2 Use the larger drill to make a hole 1 cm. ($\frac{3}{8}$ in.) deep
in the centre of the straight end. Drill a second hole in
the front of the head. Push into it a short length of
dowel for the nose.

3 The legs (one piece). Saw off a piece of thick dowel
10 cm. (4 in.) long. Drill a hole with the larger drill in
the centre of one end. At 1 cm. ($\frac{3}{8}$ in.) from the other
end drill another hole through from one side of the legs
to the other. (Diagram **b** shows the legs from the side.)

4 At 15 mm. ($\frac{5}{8}$ in.) from the same end, use the larger
drill to make a hole through from front to back of the
legs. (Diagram **c** shows the legs from the front.)

5 Hold the legs in the vice and saw a slot down to
the second hole, **c**. Clean the edges with the rasp.
Round the end with the rasp (diagram **b**).

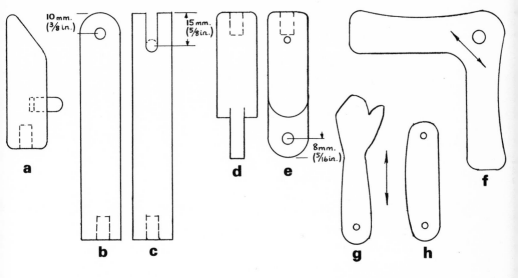

10 mm.
(⅜ in.)

15 mm.
(⅝ in.)

8mm.
(⁵⁄₁₆in.)

a

b   c   d   e   f   g   h

6 The body. Saw off a piece of dowel 18 mm. ($\frac{3}{4}$ in.) long.

7 Drill a hole in the centre at one end, using the larger drill.

8 At the opposite end saw a tongue, or tenon, 18 mm. ($\frac{3}{4}$ in.) deep and a little over 6 mm. ($\frac{1}{4}$ in.) wide. (Diagram **d** shows the front view.)

9 Round off the ends with the rasp. (Diagram **e** shows the side view.)

10 Use the larger drill to make a hole through the tenon at 8 mm. ($\frac{5}{16}$ in.) from the end, **e**.

11 Use the smaller drill to make a hole through the body 12 mm. ($\frac{1}{2}$ in.) from the top.

12 Fit the tenon in the slot in the legs and push a piece of dowel through the holes. Adjust with the rasp if necessary until there is full movement in the joint, yet leaving it stiff enough to remain fixed in any position.

13 Draw the outline of the feet, **f**, on the pinewood strip and saw close to the outline. Trim with the knife.

14 Use the larger drill to make a hole in the centre of the angle, **f**.

15 Draw the outline of the arms, **g** and **h**, on the lath. Draw two of each piece. Saw them roughly to shape. Trim the outlines with the knife.

16 Use the smaller drill to make holes through where shown. Sandpaper all parts smooth.

17 Use pieces of medium dowel to fit the head to the body and the body to the feet.

18 Use thin dowel for the shoulder and elbow joints.

19 Paint all the parts except the dowels. Assemble the pieces, using dowels in the usual way. All joints should be stiff yet adjustable.

Jewelry

Many woods need only a smooth finish and a high polish to bring out their beauty of grain and colour. Rosewood and walnut are good for colour, and pine, fir, larch and cedar for decorative grain.

Holding the knife
Hold your thumb against the work for greater control when cutting towards you.

Hold both thumbs against the knife to give greater control for the forward cuts.

Shaping
Shape each piece of jewelry and file it smooth while still attached to the stick.

Tools you need
coping saw; knife
half round rasp; vice
riffler (see page 8)
sandpaper sticks
sandpaper, coarse and fine
drills
glue (Evo-Stik or UHU)
clear varnish and brush

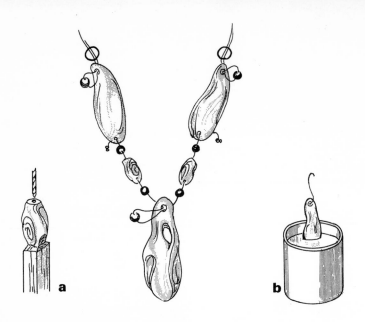

Necklace (colour photograph page 52)
Choose wood with strong grain markings 20 × 2.5 ×
  1.2 cm. (8 × 1 × ½ in.)

1 Hold the wood in the vice and, working at one end, make a hollow cut with the rasp on each face and on all edges. See which side produces the most interesting pattern.

2 Blend the forms together and draw onto them the outline of a large bead (see top beads, centre diagram).

3 Cut to shape with the knife, but leave attached to the stick. Finish shaping and sandpaper smooth.

4 Drill a tiny hole (1.5 mm. or $\frac{1}{16}$ in. diameter) at each end of the bead before sawing it off the stick and finishing the end with rasp and sandpaper.

5 Make a second bead of a similar shape, but with a different grain pattern.

6 Make the bottom bead. Vary its shape by drilling a hole off centre and rounding the edges.

8 Cut the smaller beads in the same way, but drill a hole right through from the top, diagram **a**.

9 Give all beads a coat of varnish. Sandpaper smooth when quite dry.

10 For the finishing coat of varnish, push a piece of wire through the hole in each bead. Dip it in the varnish, **b**, and hang to dry.

11 When threading the necklace, add a smaller gold bead between the wooden ones. This will help the necklace to hang well.

Snake brooch (colour photograph page 52)
Use medium hard wood with a decorative grain
    5 × 2.5 cm. × 9 mm. (6 × 1 × ⅜ in.)

1 Draw the outline onto one end of the wood. Leaving the tail end fixed, saw to the outline.

2 Commence shaping with the knife by cutting a chamfer on all edges, back and front.

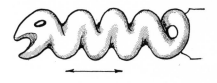

3 Starting from the head, shape the coils to a round section. Make a hollow section between the coils with a riffler.

4 Smooth with sandpaper sticks and finish with fine sandpaper.

5 Drill holes for mouth and tail.

6 Saw off from the stick and finish the end. Varnish as for necklace. Glue on a brooch pin.

Snake pendant

Use a piece of wood
   12 cm. × 4 cm. × 9 mm.
   ($4\frac{3}{4}$ × $1\frac{1}{2}$ × $\frac{3}{8}$ in.)

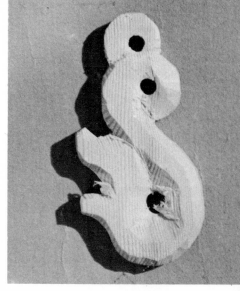

1 Draw the outline on the wood and drill the holes. Use a 3 mm. ($\frac{1}{8}$ in.) drill.

2 Saw round the outline with a coping saw, leaving the head end attached.

3 With the knife, chamfer all edges, back and front. Cut deeper where the coils overlap on the front.

4 Round all the edges with riffler and sandpaper sticks. Shape the hole at the back of the head with knife and riffler.

5 Separate from stick. Sandpaper smooth and varnish as for necklace.

Owl brooch (Photograph page 52)
Use wood 8 × 6 × 1 cm. (3$\frac{1}{4}$ × 2$\frac{1}{2}$ × $\frac{3}{8}$ in.)

1 Draw the outline on the wood.

2 Drill four 6 mm. ($\frac{1}{4}$ in.) diameter holes where indicated. These will help in cutting the outline.

3 Saw close to the outline.

4 Chamfer round the drilled holes, the top of the head, and all round the face.

5 Cut a hollow down the wings and shape the body with knife and half round rasp.

6 Finish the outline with knife and round file.

7 Chamfer the front edges of the wings. Chamfer all round the back outline to reduce the thickness at the edges.

8 Sandpaper smooth and varnish. Glue a brooch pin across the back.

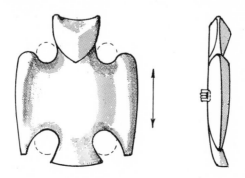

Now you have solved these tangrams, you may like to try some more. There are plenty of ideas in *Tangrams: 330 puzzles* by Ronald C. Read, published by Dover in America and Constable in Britain.

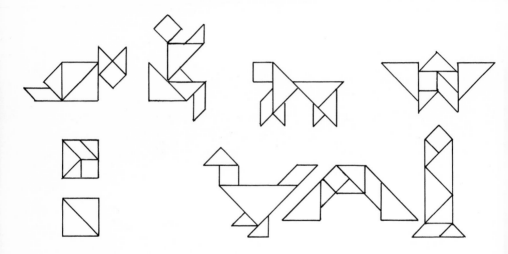

Glossary

chamfer

a bevel; a sloping cut on an edge

chip-carving

the cutting of 'V'-shaped notches or grooves in the surface of the wood

radius

a curve; part of the circumference of a circle joining two straight lines or surfaces

to scribe

to draw with a tool

seasoned wood

wood which has been stored for a sufficient length of time to allow the moisture content to evaporate

templet

described under the heading of 'Making a templet' on page 10. A ruler would become a templet when used to draw a straight line and a coin would become a templet when used as a guide for drawing a circle

tenon

a square piece of wood made to fit into a square hole to form a joint. In the case of the woodpecker, the tenon is rounded off into a dowel

whittling

cutting thin slices or shavings from the surface of the wood

Index